"Steve Gerson's latest collection moves from light to dark. It begins with the kind of love poems that could only be written by someone who has loved for a long time. They are rife with powerful images that show us true love doesn't have to fade: "your hands in mine as small as birdsong" or "stay with me as long as ink and paper remember." In part two, Gerson shatters us with images of loss like "seawater salt, like acid rains, eroded her resolve into fissures" or "like planting corn in concrete." The final section of the book, "Lost," takes the reader through the experience of various speakers who suffer trauma. Throughout the book, Gerson experiments with form, most notably with the erasure poems in the "Lost" section. This book begins with bird song, but it ends with an AK 47 and the Apocalypse. This great collection of poems is a knockout."

-Dr. Beth Gulley, author of *I Am Your Fish Drowning In Air: Love Poems*

"Albeit an optimist, this poet writes truthfully about the trying times we have all been living through. Recently, we have been forced to make frequent pivots — pivots to plans, to rules, to procedures, to hopes, to change. Love and losing and loss are the felt arc of this chapbook. This poetic arc suggests continued inspiration for the next phase — finding peace and love and hopefully solutions beyond the madness. Gerson writes, "but overflowing onto pages into our future written" in Chapter 1. These words hint at a positive conclusion beyond Chapter 3."

-Dr. Stefani G. Buchwitz, Director, Self Graduate Fellowship, University of Kansas

"Steve Gerson's evocative poems immerse the reader in what it means to love in our unsettling times. The first of three sections, "Love," transitions from the enclosed and timeless world of the lover and his beloved to our present-day, digital world where a love letter, no longer handwritten, can be deleted in an instant. "Losing," the middle chapter, begins with classic impediments to love: unfaithfulness, lack of communication, illness. The intrusions in "Lost" switch from the personal to the world at large: homelessness, racism, climate change, 9/11, Covid, and hanging over it all, the digital world which we have embraced. Throughout, striking images highlight the progression from love to loss as the poems move from the beloved, "your hands ...as small as birdsong" to a bride wearing "toxic mascara" to a teacher, "a little lady wearing a reindeer sweater" and wielding a gun. Timely and thought-provoking, energetic and perceptive, Gerson's poems are a testament to the challenges love faces in our viral world."

-Edie Cottrell Kreisler, Professor Emeritus of
English, Merritt College, Oakland, CA.

"This second volume of rhythmic incantations cements Steve Gerson's standing as a foremost American poet. Exuding sensuousness, pathos, and prescience, *Viral: Love and Losses in the Time of Insanity* brilliantly captures the urban landscape amid the pandemic as expertly as its counterpart, *Once Planed Straight*, evokes enduring images of the heartland. Gracefully and poignantly etched, *Viral* contains fifty-two exquisitely drawn poems nested in the pristine arcs of "Love," "Losing," and "Lost." The braided themes range from enduring love to vaccine refuseniks to the national shame of school shootings involving 'another child another child,' as Gerson eloquently weeps."

-Dr. Robert Cottrell, author of *Izzy: A Biography
of I.F. Stone*

Viral:
Love and Losses in
the Time of Insanity

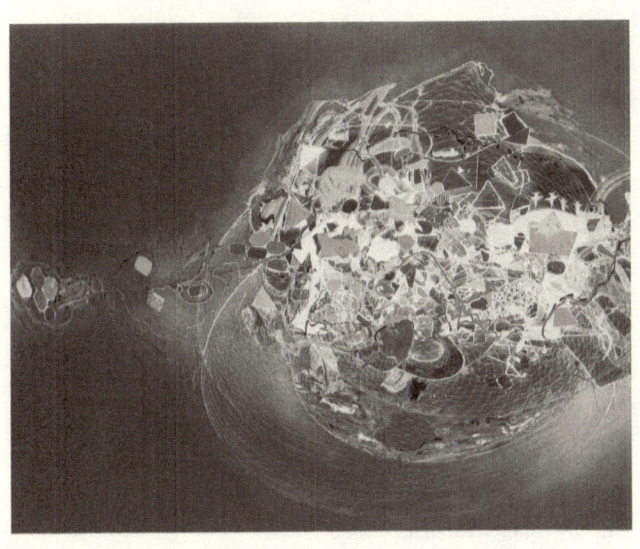

Poems by Steve Gerson

Spartan
Press

Spartan Press

Kansas City, MO

spartanpress.com

Spartan
Press

Copyright © Steve Gerson, 2022

First Edition: 1 3 5 7 9 10 8 6 4 2

ISBN: 978-1-958182-10-9

LCCN: 2022940192

Author photo (with family): Stefani Buchwitz

Cover art (c) Copyright 2022, "Duplicity," Larry Thomas

Cover art photographed by Tom Tarnowski

Cover art archivist Collin Thomas

Title page image (c) Copyright 2022, "Blithe Betrayal," Larry Thomas

Acknowledgments

Special thanks to the editors of these publications where some of the poems in this book first appeared:

"I touch the touch of you," / *Dots Publication.*
"(My Want) and This It Seems," "Self Portrait as November," "Self Portrait as Disease" "The Walk,"/ *The Decadent Review,* "In the Time of Letters," "OXY," "Divorce Proceedings, Case #2029," "The Weight of Want," "The Other," "Erased," "Semaphore\Distress," "Beneath the soil but still, lamentations on aging." "Soundless Screaming in the Nothingness of Your Space." / *In Parentheses,* "Improvisation" / *Lucky Jefferson,* "Hurricane," / *Elevation Review,* "Salt into nectar," "Moan" "Redacted"/ *Route 7 Review,* "Wreckage, Relent—a Sonnet" "!not," / *The Rainbow Poems UK,* "Modern Romance," "Dementia,"/ *Scapegoat,* "Ingesting eclipses," / *Abstract,* "Dissipate," "Black Stones," / *Panoplyzine,* "Shrieking" / *The Write Launch,* "Like planting corn in concrete," / *Crack the Spine,* "Even a sip to cleanse" / *Constellations,* "Refugee," "Olvidado"/ *Antonym,* "3 a.m" / *Indolent Review,* "Was" / / *White Wall Review,* "Phantom Pain: Afghanistan, December 12, 2018, 11:01 GMT" / *Poets Reading the News,* "breathing underwater . . . a Vet returns to Norfolk" / *Novus Literary Journal,* "PTSD," / *The Dillydoun Review,* "Shrill" / *Red Ogre Review,* "The Lord's Prayer, Version 2.0"/ *Toe Good.*

Table of Contents

Chapter 1 Love

Chapter 2 Losing

Chapter 3 Lost

The 2020s: Madness!

The 2020s: Madness! Viral tweets from unhinged "leaders."
Viral viruses from bats and pigs and people. Viral murders
of people of color at the hands of people in blue. Viral hand-
held photos from marauders in the Capitol. Supply chain
disruptions, mask mandates (unheeded), rampant racism,
travelers on planes attacking flight attendants, businesses
shuttered, children caged at the borders, children murdered
in their elementary schools, families isolated from families,
deaths. Rants, refusals, reprisals . . . ruin.

This chapbook is divided into three chapters: love, losing,
lost.

The book isn't a historical rendering; it's a visceral response
to tragic times. The book responds to shared pain but also
celebrates love in the time of insanity.

I'm hopeful, but I'm scared, and I bet you feel the same.

For Sharon,

Yes

what sound was that at night
the sigh of a door opening
what light spoke from dark interiors
what sight did two eyes meet
from distances and draw close
did hands touch did thought reach
across and think maybe now
this time is now did the questions answer
yes we answered yes and answer still

Chapter 1 Love

He touched each finger of her hand. Slowly tracing the skin, knuckles, the webs between the thumb and forefinger, middle, and each finger after. Rising toward her fingertips. Falling back to her palm where he settled softly. He circled her wrist with his fingers, seeking the pulse in the dark room beneath their sheet in the quiet of their night . . . safe.

I touch the touch of you

I touch the touch of you
and sing your pulse
and feel your feelings
inside (my heart) the hardness

of my bones, softened
by your softness as a thought
of breezes on leaves quickening
along (inside) my veins,

your hands in mine
as small as birdsong,
the treble of tremors,
and I travel your body,

touch on touch,
your contours (rounding)
fig-sweet
and you, if so open,

(my heart) allow breath
hurry, breathing, breathless,
more alive in and with
the touch of you

(My Want) and This It Seems

1.

and this it seems (can't you tell),
that I in all things, need and weary,
reach, as lips seek air, and then there
rises you (my want)

2.

to be as if (to see and sound)
the sound of your dreams, arms
and face, reaching to sing no secret,
you (my want)

3.

now and next (into ever then),
we beginning (as seed to flower),
our becoming (as bud to branch),
to find, always, you

(my want) and this it seems

In the Time of Letters

when love was a word
written with a trembling hand
and folded to keep emotions
embraced on lines plumbed
the pen pressed ink as
tongues touching to imprint
perhaps I had just left or
was on the way my words
to say in loops like pulse
stay with me for me as long as
ink and paper remember then
you'd return blue lines your veins
on paper to yellow in time as
time permits the words a promise
not to be deleted as TikTok or
clickbait text ephemeral data overload
digitized love but overflowing
onto pages into our future written

Improvisation

A thrust of upbeat tempo sends shudders
that pulse like bass beat thrums

fingers and thumb as hands along your back
each bone a note my body sings and zing

the bend of riff your sway into my arms' embrace
I feel your breath and sigh the melody stretching

giving going our love and sensuously your name in song
from my lips sips as saxophone wails and funk pop drop

then the drumming of tap and brush along your shoulders
the snap of snares like birds caught on wing we entangled

in with of our palms intertwined heat hard and skin soft
your voice the croon as from a wine-soaked microphone

my call and response we in syncopated dance our harmonic
discordance of jangling notes aligning misaligned

quaver along the staff of clef sharp breath mark trill and turn
slurring accented up bow down bow my fingers through your hair

Beneath the soil but still, lamentations
on aging

In the emptiness of a dry season
when wind creaks through brittle
leaves beneath the creased soil more
sand than silt always seeds of passion
warm and wait as fingers probe as palms
caress.

Spring rains have ceased. Summer heat has withered.
Fall grayness suffocates to numbness. Yet despite
yet even through yet a current flows subterranean
like memory and waits as fingers probe as palms
caress.

The winter tree is bent with pods pale around the
trunk laid bare under a darkening sky under skyless clouds.
In the stillness of a late season, roots still dig deep
through clay for love's wetness as fingers probe as palms
caress.

There's desiccation in the flesh as leaves fall and blow
across the brown ground. But leaves pirouette in dance
and chime on ice dreaming to rise and reunite with trees
in spring green renewed as fingers probe and palms
caress.

Love Devouring Time

In this late day of sunset nearing night,
When fingers ache like breaking winter ice,
When eyes glaze and yellowing letters blur,
I hunger for you with a young man's heart.

In the shadow of darkening corners,
Where sight won't see and reach's stumble fetters,
Where memory clouds as a haloed moon,
I hunger for you like streams seeking flume.

Touching your skin, I hunger for your need
As to taste the tang of pomegranate seeds,
Your sharp and round loveliness, light from dark,
Your body each venture a voyage embarked.

In my hunger, the hands of time unwind.
Your love I devour, devouring time.

A Continent of Two

We in one another's arms,
our contours combine to make mounds and lakes,
to shield and shelter.

Our love forms continents,
created between our interstices, sufficing
though the world, of course, encroaches.

In our union, our island nation
of bed, home, harbor, and heartstone,
we populate against populations,
containing in our two multitudes.

Earth riles, rife with dissension and insensitivities,
but sunrise to moonset still
within our embrace,
our arms entwining.

OXY

I remember her toes pointing skyward on our yard swing,
her hair aswirl in tendrils, a young girl's light leaping the
breeze, our hopes for her future ensnared in a parent's web
like a struggling moth.

Between her springtime ponytail tossed in play, catching
the dusk of sunshine dimming, and her goth cut later blackened
by shadows creeping in cliches, the weight of mold dampening
roses, her synapses frayed, sheared ragged with a dull blade.

She was an egret soaring low above a lake, her grey reflection on
the water breaking the white of fragile feathers. She flew from the
swing and fell, an October leaf, its color bleached in winter dull,
and medicated depressing pain, deferring a future of relapses.

I could not find her in the branches hissing on the chill winds.
I could not revive the darkening rose or unravel the tangled moth.
The light that played upon her like whispered tunes hushed, and
I am not consoled.

Hurricane

The winds began at 10 p.m.
As shoreline sands rose and whipped

And surf stirred in roiling pitch
The spit of sea and furling flags.

I'll need help to latch the slats
And lay down bags against the surge

Said Dad, and I leapt to aid
Grabbing candles and flame

And towels to staunch swollen streets.
Then wait. A storm wakes and roars

In pace set by pressures barometric
As seas suck sky and cloud cover cycles.

By 3 a.m. the gale whined
Like nails driven into coffin pine

Like unhinged screws ripped from screens
When swirling spout streamed from sea

Tornadic howl and empty eye air
soulless as the demon Aamon

Funnel teeth and trident tongue.
Our house shook as windows shattered,

A 2x4 impaled our roof
And outside wind rained indoors.

Dive for the bed said Dad, he
Our raft as we rode the storm till

It wore out, leaving debris, our
Sensibilities adrift as shredded sails.

salt into nectar

trailing sorrow like the cry of gulls you
part the curtains diaphanous with rain
marsh reeds the color of rust and despair

soddening your walk toward the beach
sandals unlaced footprints dispelling
in seaweed as you slip deeply into

seabed churn your funereal brain
suffocating as undertow growls grasp
you gasping tears surging from submerged

swell the hollow of your eyes breath held
depleting light through the surf a memory
of children laughing on a sun-lit beach

help me reach beneath the waves releasing
you from riptide bog and draw you onto land
replacing tidewrack and dark depth with lavender

and marigold replacing the shriek of sea birds
with the thrum of bees the salt from your tears
turned to nectar to dapple your face with honey

You in the sound of seagull shrieks

A torrent of roars, fractious waves crash into broken
jetties as harmonic drones, drawn by the moon's

plaintive moan along thrown sand. A murmur
of embrace, sea foam caresses the shoreline, reaching

through tide wrack, undertow churn. Seagulls shriek
and cycle labyrinthine above surf grinding grains

of sharded shells. In the distance, fishermen cast
seines into dark sea swells buffeted by winter winds,

searching. I stand on a pier, neither sea nor sand,
black in anorak, roped by pilings

and the distance of distant horizons, grey green
waters scribing blue grey sky, while seagulls harangue,

clamoring accusations, and wheel and wheedle
above waves retreating seaward. And I yearn for you.

Wreckage, Relent—a Sonnet

she lost him on a Wednesday evening
pandemic shattered against dusk November gray
her wreckage like flown crows' exploding wings
now what she asked, how to see beyond today

the hollow sky above her deep dry well
how to escape the wind worrying through
worm-holed wood with discordant flute calls
how to claw out, find footing, head raised anew

breathe, he said, in, out, in again, out again
accept, rebuild, accept, rebuild each sigh
unraveled threads knitted, shredded steel melding,
repairing birds' wings to glide if not to fly

downdrafts become upswells as todays beget
tomorrows, flight when gray and dusk relent

You spoke but I didn't hear

you spoke but I didn't hear
my eyes shrouded your lips pursed
distant as stone a tombed weeping angel
and I became
a leaf flown south in the winter
blown into a swirl
a fallen seedling adrift left fetal
curling on the stone
rootless as a shadow
our miscommunication
rootless as a shadow
curling on the stone
a fallen seedling adrift left fetal
blown into a swirl
a leaf flown south in the winter
and I became
distant as stone a tombed weeping angel
my eyes shrouded your lips pursed
you spoke but I didn't hear

Modern Romance

She wore toxic mascara.
It scribed her face in icicles
when she cried, often.
She filed her nails
into penknives to carve
down his back, his chest, his arms, his face
in romance, in anger, as often.
He bathed in Agent Orange.
It wafted from him as mephitis
from sulfurous sinkholes.
His pointed, steel-toe stingray
boots, sharpened on acid,
bit into her with each embrace.
They married when the wind
screamed, guests applauding
their divorce.

Chapter 2 Losing

The October wind worried the trees, already leafless in anticipation of November freezes. The trees shook. Birds, their feathers fluffed for warmth, gripped the branches tightly. The moon was rising quickly, diminishing in size as it sped skyward. Cloud cover increased.

Soundless Screaming in the Nothingness of Your Space

When you stole
into the room
like an eclipse,
your halfmoon eyes
hiding behind
asteroids crashing,
I knew what you'd say,
saying,
"I'm seeing someone else,"
my feet unearthed,
zero gravity free fall
swallowing my screams
soundless in the nothingness
of your space.

Dementia

At first her pauses were commas,
synapses between now and next,
uncertainties, ellipses waiting
for closure, her mind only partly
cloudy with sunlight seeking sky
like a sentence ending, expecting
the next capital letter, but in time.
stops. lingered. longer. longing.
Now, her gauze-eyed gaze brackets
air; her words stumble in syntax
shards, muffling screams; her steps
stutter shuddering like inverted
exclamation points¡¡¡

Ingesting eclipses

1.

We consume darkness in loss, ingesting eclipses.
When earth and moon fail to syncopate, our axis askew,
Truth becomes dross. Even gilding fails to validate.

2.

Heat-steeped cement, iridescent, turns vapor to flame.
A leaf on the ground colors Fall, mocking with vibrancy.
Mirages fail to satiate, quenching with aridity.

3.

There's no reckoning a mind's cyclonic confusion.
Though we assume, destiny downdrafts in rotating winds.
Clouds move north and south; cicadas siren suffering.

Dissipate

Your tongue tied knotting a cherry stem
You speak to me in cuneiform
Reading like a lead pencil on black paper
Footprints on snow white on white
A screaming contrail sky written
We disconnect, dissipating in air streams

Shrieking

She called,
the phone shrieking,
a warped door creaking shut.
"It's over . . . finally."
The cancer cachectic,
his cells oozing like snails salted,
his 6'2" high school linebacker's frame
now a wicker-backed bentwood rocker,
his Vietnam sergeant's bark
muffled to a morphine moan.
Laughing, "Remember how he'd say,
'I want to die on the front nine,
my backswing rising.'
Remember his laugh,
cognac-smoky, unfiltered Camel chortle.
Remember how he'd toss us high,
shelter our lows,
his forearms knotted from cleaving
shoulder bones from the chuck."
It's raining when I talk to her,
the rain prattling innocence.

Moan

in
your
absence
I
despair
of
breath
as
air
bubbles
burst
from
the
moan
of
whale
songs

Like planting corn in concrete

escaping the sun cataract from coal plumes
fleeing pesticides leaching landforms
eluding wetlands crystalline from dying clouds

the shadow elongated by halogen
   stilled
      stalking
         stopped
now sprints for the garage wall

claws clicking like thrown seeds on the underground asphalt
the tan blur of accordion ribs
    flashes toward movement
       leaping after the prey
          plastic blown by a cornered draft

the bag snared in yellowed teeth
    shaking
       tearing
         spitting out
the coyote pants in its cement habitat
displaced between parked cars

Even a sip to cleanse

I'm parched
dry as kindling

crumbling as decayed leaf fall
skin peeling sawn into dust

24/7 newscasts sirocco plumes
enflame my brain in shrill tweets

stinging my tearless eyes with ash
my ears clogged in racist rant

instagram impinging Kardashian flashing
wikilooping clickbaits reptilian brain tik tok

my tongue wooden with viral screams
the world swirls shredded sand shifting

everything overturned it's water I need
a pail a rainbow of concentric circles

from dew drops to quench to swab
my eyes my ears my throat flash bang gassed

even a sip to cleanse what aches
my labored breathing

Divorce Proceedings, Case #2029

Barometric pressure twisting between invective and indifference, he, for her, was like breathing the hot dry air of Arizona, scalding, his heat an acetylene torch in her throat, like breathing swamp humidity in Louisiana, each breath breathless, so her lungs strained, gasping like a beached fish, gill quivered. Loveless, his arms withheld from her as if he were a Greek statue lopped limbless by marauding infidels stealing her belief. She had tried standing tall on Doric columns, their filigreed flutes and fillets her fragile strength, but he, like seawater salt, like acid rains, eroded her resolve into fissures, and she, as glass blown in fire and air, a bowl to carry water, blue as sustenance, stream fed, shattered under his burden, water evaporating into rock dry sand.

Refugee

Leaving
tree shards
ashen streets
angry fists
cadaverous consciences
Sofia Perdido arrived August 17
to a land green with promise.
Homeless
tempest-tossed
words unfamiliar fell upon her
as suffocating leaves sodden black.
Skies corn blue as her Guatemalan flag glared.
Sunlight grew shadows.
Sofia
transplanted in a new world
hungered unfed
heard unheard
touched untouched
saw unseen
opportunity.

The Weight of Want

When Covid closed the café, 12th and Main, where I
    bussed tables
and took orders, $7.29 an hour and found, the boss said,
    "No problem,
Sid, we'll be back soon, but for now I need to let you go."
    No problem

my ass, me with the two kids and Mary long gone. I left,
    the juke
moaning "I can't get no," and trudged home, my gold work
    shirt splattered
with ketchup, my hair grill fire grease streaked, as if clawed
    by predators,

the whole world a wolf's howl, but I could keep the kids
    fed and
the rent paid, barely, spooning up beans and Wonder
    Bread heels
as hard as shoe tongues, watered-down milk and stale
    cereal, into

the night's hollow like an empty well, mending their thrift
    store clothes
with thread-thin wishes. Now, eight months into the
    pandemic, the diner
only at half shift, my unemployment check dissipating like
    a retreating

contrail from my damned senator's departing jet, no
  stimulus
package passed, I sit at my kitchen table consuming bills,
  facing
affliction, eviction, both kids starting to cough, their
  wheezes like

air from flattening tires. Lines in my face etch deeper with
  each click
of the clock's second hand, each tick a nail hammered into
  coffins.
I feel the weight of want, head bowed heavy to the pull of
  earth's gravity.

Black Stones

Roberto *y* Jesus, *dos hermanos,* left the scorched
fields of Saltillo like sand swirling in a dry heat,
Roberto *con* six pesos and a pocket of cornmeal.

Jesus carried a liter Coke bottle of water. They
travelled toward Piedras Negras at the Texas border
near Eagle Pass, following coyote paths

through the Chihuahuan Desert, through
saguaro thorns and hollow bones, through
El Rio, the river's rocks clawing their

feet like *El Chupacabra*, pooling their
Mexican blood on bitter soil, threading
ICE and armed home guard, cresting buttes

under vulture eyes, climbing barbed fences,
slicing their skin, entangling their hopes.
"Podemos hacerlo. 'Berto.

Te cubro la espalda, como siempre.
Grab hol' of my shoulders, *ese."*
They sought family in Dodge City, 700 miles

north toward Eldorado, sun flamed, wind worried,
where the brothers could work the meat plants, gutting
livestock, cadaverous eyes reflecting sterile walls,

and travel east to Wichita to cut cotton and
harvest milo, bent backed under the weight
of wearied bags, then north again

to Kansas City for apple picking, stepping
on cores that cracked like nails pounded
into caskets, migrating with the seasons.

They patched their clothes with baling string,
quenched their thirst with rainbows, heel-bruised
walked the black stones in search of America.

Pleasant Meadows, Improving the Quality of Your Life

Start your life in luxury protect your family with steel pipes
and lead paint ensure their safety with space-age fire
    retardant
asbestos ceiling tiles and insulation read the 5th Avenue ads
promoting life in Pleasant Meadows rising above the city's
    skyline
in clustered concrete

I wish the falling stairs rose at the housing project and reached
sunlight cool breezes fresh air yearning at Pleasant Meadows
so named by absentee landlords secure in acres of gardens
    and sculpted
topiaries their suburban children playing lawn tennis and
    riding
miniature ponies the Meadows' barred

metal stairs choke and descend onto rubble cratered cement
    bottle
shards and ripped condoms kids playing hopscotch around
    chalk
corpses spin the bottle with discarded pints of Johnny Red
    and Jim
Beam tidily winks with rusted needles on asphalt the sole bare
patch of Meadows' garden a coffin

shaped planter rigged from crate slats fertilized by cigarette butts

growing dried vines and one rotting tomato stunted from
    fractured
sunlight reflecting off glass slivers wind moaning through
    the project's
stairwells hollow as whining marrowless bones broken teeth
    whimpering
of rent aspirations

Enter the monitor

Leave behind the sound of birds,
Rustling winds, skin on skin.
Foster virtual cats with hats;
Befriend BFF emoji hearts.

Let your looking glass
Reflect only inward
Where you post for likes,
A thumbs up to slake your thirst

Rather than a bistro merlot
Or swirling macchiato
Shared across a tabletop,
Words warming the interstice.

There's such comfort in a blog's
Self-embrace. "I tap, I scroll,"
Your digital native's memoir
Memorializing Descartes.

Burrow in online;
Fight off the world's chill
With cyber hibernation into
An internet continent.

Turn your back to the living room.
Enter the monitor.

Darkness Lightening

I'm tired   tired of the darkness
dry kindling   dead leaf fall
the dark stinging my skin
with viral spores

parched   in the dry night
my throat clogged   with clods of rant
shrouding my voice
muffled

stumbling   through this darkness
bruised on clickbait brambles   pursued by
   shrieking tweets
stepping on stones
seeking water to soothe my thirst

seeking light   there
there in my path   concentric circles of light
rainbowing
I see as if a pail dew-fed
to quench to swab my eyes my throat

flash bang gassed   a sip to cleanse
my labored breathing   and hungering

I cup my hands as in prayer and
kneel to drink

Olvidado

Each day before dawn
To escape her husband's fists   his knuckles stropped
   sharp by her bones
Maria Olvidado reached for the sea

Each day the sea's undertow stared

Each day before he rose
Exhausted from ministering   his liquor-stewed justice
She asked the sea for answers

Each day the sea's undertow glared

Each day before returning to husband Hector
She cleansed in the sand   sunrise bruised
She appeased in the sea's mist

Each day the sea's undertow looked seaward

Each day before the next day
Maria sailed Hector's nightly bottle   to fathom
The sea's destiny on a distant beach

Each day the sea's undertow invited

Air Quality

When 9-11 struck, it didn't affect me in the least,
vile to say. I was thousands of miles away.

From the distance of my TV set, I saw the planes
insert themselves onto the screens and watched

the horror on distant faces, tearstained soot and
bloodstained clothes, victims choking on fire and

ash. They held to friends or passersby, their weeping
eyes compassionate, supporting each other against the

shock, their shared attack from ideological threat,
the sirens wailing in their ears.   I ate my cereal and

went to work, embraced some friends in hollow hugs.
"Terrible, huh? You ok? Want to grab some lunch today?"

I jogged that noon under blue skies, breathing in clean air,
the fires raging somewhere else. No terrorists strolled

my neighborhood. Now, terrorists are in the air, aerosols
they're called, I hear, virus spores expelled in coughs. Who

needs an army when you have a sleeve? I jogged today and
kept my distance, six feet out, no hugs allowed in sympathy.

I breathed in but what inhaled? Each breath I took virulent
motes, angry as warrior wasps, sucked into my bronchial

tubes. I passed another walking by.   She edged away, shunning
my presence, fearfully eyeing my viable threat. I could be
   carrying

coronas in my breath, my hands, my chest. "Don't breathe
   near, don't
touch, don't share," she and I at microbial war, fighting for
   quality air.

He's got the whole world

His wife stashed in the kitchen with the blender
the kids stacked on the couch by last month's magazines

a TV shouting ads for uppers downers sexual satisfaction aids
a sleep dreaming dog moaning for its mate

debris from remote planets
sounds inaudible in his space

He is mesmerized massaging his handheld
coaxing its communication with e-friends

caressing the monitor to touch a message deleted
stroking the screen to scroll through Hulu and Sling TV

episodes of loving families pixilated
his present micro thin flat screen pocket-sized

Self Portrait as November

As November, between Corpus and Pensacola,
Gulf Coast, the sun has inhaled

in a sigh, and the memory of summer, an undertow,
darkens the murky sea, dredged in riptides.

The sky is green with sea mist. Gray cloud cover
cowers. Gulls wheel and screech, black

against the gray clouds, commas punctuating the sky
in endless stammering, sentences without verbs.

Oysters among the jetties gulp soiled silt.
A swarm of mosquitos whispers,

hissing like tar steaming.
My chest heaves, the air heavy

with the scent of crab carapaces and webs of strewn
seaweed littering the sand. I've become the coast.

I've become November. I've become invertebrate.
My mouth tastes of salt, my fingernails,

like waves breaking on shore, claw
and question submerging.

Chapter 3 Lost

The door was shut. The 60-watt bulb above the door was burned out and had not been replaced. The dark room was still with dead air.

3 a.m.

I see evening all day, 3 a.m. every hour,
and the day's night sounds like dissonance,
a dream distorted to blue and black.

In the nightly day, I run fearful streets,
looking back on crows flying crooked
through slanted air, a house with vortex windows,

the door a jagged maw, a dog moaning, its flaming fleas
dancing a derelict jig. Heat sizzles into cold, expiring
on darkness like a moon's corona behind a constant cloud.

Was

through the door   the bed
once with two warm furrows   is wintered
covers tightly sealed   comforter creaseless as ice
pillows aligned at right angles   shuttered like boards
    squared
I sleep in another room   now

Self Portrait as Disease

In the disease of age and happenstance,
darkness extends a companion hand,
the dry cough of covetous crows,
the wheeze of bats in blackening throes.
I feel my face shriek-stained and slackening,
a Daliesque clock with numbers fading.

I crouch between the next I fear
and failure to recall what disappeared
behind moonless nights where shadows hide,
cloud-sheared skies and crushing tides,
a virus here, an opiate there,
contagion combusting like forested fire.

I had a friend who lost his wife
who lost her way through dementia, her strife
the gauze-eyed gaze of bracketed air,
and he lost too to cachexia,
the cancerous wrench of breathless churr
between the stork's perch and buzzard's soar.

And they and I and you and this,
our darkening age of mosquitos' hiss
in pooled waters quenching less
beneath tearing winds and treelessness,
intubation, divisive skies,
I fear this disease will anesthetize.

The Other

It slouches from the west, slithering as sunlight dims,
and casts darkness, a vortex of reason churning with
gnashed teeth, anarchy of truncheons assuaged in angry
tweets from leafless trees. This shadow, plagues of beasts
and the spilled blood of first born, promulgates pain
upon the other. The other, those far from the center,
as rings of dust around a spinning sphere. The other,
flung to the ground, foot upon their necks, strangle held
and breathless in the weight of ether thinned. Who watches
the wince, phone filmed? Who judges the slouching beast?

Erased

The steaming grate near the bridge wheezed warm air
against the December cold so I claimed
it as home unfurling my cardboard cover
and newspaper sheets reporting Dow gains

unpacking my shredded BDUs and jug
of Johnny Red next to my camo field gear
my purple heart hanging like smudged clotted blood
I had fought for land before as squad leader

3rd Marines Desert Storm urging twelve brothers
toward smoke and sand commanding resources
not sufficient for a resume so war
for god and country led to life under bridges

rat squeals rough coughs dumpster food and sleep on grates
my face etched from hot metal like strafed scars

Phantom Pain: Afghanistan,
December 12, 2018, 11:01 GMT

On a wet day in a land mostly dry,
on a day dimmed where life normally glared,
our 12-man squadron was decimated.
I walked point, a two-by-two formation,
through a valley slice. "Incoming!" First whine,
then scream, the air singed, creosote acrid,
land roiling, men thrown skyward combusting,
shrapnel blown from a gnarled hand as petals
through limbs, severed then, cauterizing next.
Concussed, minutes, moments later, I saw
eleven depressions where men once lived.
Now, PTSD cracked, I carry them:
Day, my prosthetic pounding nails in nerves;
Night, my stump jolting, they my phantom pain.

breathing underwater . . . a Vet returns to Norfolk

from the overlook   wind flowers
          the tufted marsh reeds
reefed by crab dunes   as undertows weep
                    the shoreline
into uncertainty
          salt scouring illusion

low clouds turn gray   fraught with green mist
          caught in an upswell
                    from heavy surf
and the rumble   of distant lightning
surges like pulse
          in deepening   seabed churn

breath underwater bursts   sand bleeds blistering

!not

going to: follow your punctuation rules
for who you think, I am, today

a pink (gauzy) syntax
in your red/state white/male cataract

no!t going to be pastel
quiet interrupted a grl

mascara my (im)perfection wear froth
to slake your thirst your hand

holding my throat like a beer bottle
?want me to dress like something edible

a pomegranate pansy whirl of cotton candy
to sweeten teeth not going to

bend under your shard ceiling bend over
ogled an *objet d*'morsel fckd

on your testosterone timetable accept 7/10th
of a dollar my X boxed in [by your y]

not going to stay in line pirouette on cue
stand on blistered toes to reach higher

dance for your reality show government
, can't, won't:

Semaphore\Distress

! We hold down
created (un)equal
gender specific
endowed rights
(? self-evident)
that all certain men
are inalienable
pursuing life
(! can't breathe)
liberty
happiness
among others with
in\justice on their throats:

PTSD

I hear the buzz of starlings swarm
And cloud the sky in blackening drear.
Their fearful clattering in harm,
Their murmurations shriek and warn
My empty house cloaked in fear.

Each day the thousands pale and fail.
They die like shredded shrouds tear
and curtain my mind's wail
While plagues of garbled voices rail
My empty house cloaked in fear.

Wars uncivil, terror flights,
fists uplifting in despair,
The urge to love succumbs to fight
The right with words, the wrong with might,
My empty house cloaked in fear.

It's chattering of starlings crazed.
A man goes down as truncheons rear
In blood and bones and faces dazed.
Broken beaks shredding unphased,
My empty house cloaked in fear.

The Walk

Each day I wake to one less day
And fight the worm that fact is fate.
I take a step and yearn to stay.

Why look back when apples fall?
The tree is wood for coffins made.
Each day is sleep for one less day.

I feel the cold wind gray the day
So bless the ground and fight the fade.
I take a step and learn to stay.

Why stand beneath the tree's shade?
See beyond the forested maze
And wake the day though less one day.

Nature has more in play,
Light to seize the dark at bay.
I'll take a step and work to stay.

I walk steady to pace the wait.
What came far is near to pass.
Each day I wake to one less day.
I take a step and fight to stay.

Redacted

L fe periph ral in technicolor

phot synth tic green trees fabricat ng oxygen

oth rs, inebriat s of air, g lp the stuff like absinthe

their l ngs c mb st ng to fuel blo d red

rose-col r d c rp scl s upload g

others m rk time as ▮▮▮▮ white pa dl s row

churn g blu lakes into mist ris g to kiss th rm ls

▮▮▮▮ as br wn s nd grinds d wn h rglass s

you are

gone

a d I'm ▮ appendage black ni g

▮ unhealed ▮▮▮

a bl ck h le ▮▮▮ ▮▮ light crushed

a ▮▮ moon ▮▮ smudged acr s a bl ck sky

▮▮ ecl ps ing st d

A wind blew through

Monday, September 23, Grand Chenier, LA,
hurricane season. The sky was the color of silk

coffin liners. The wind was heaving, bowing
and rising as mourners in prayer, quiet then

shrieking when wailing began. Palm leaves
outside the bedroom window startled

and calmed and woke and roiled.
I sat in the bedroom and watched the storm

unfold as bible pages turning from *John's*
hearts untroubled and unafraid to *Ecclesiastes'*

dust returning to the ground. Fronds on the
wallpaper, once verdant, now grayed in the storm

shadows. The chandelier swayed in the house's
torment, casting light flickers like candles snuffed.

She was still. Only her brown hair now pewter
quivered on the pillow, a stray breeze from the window,

the curtain shivering as the hurricane descended. Others
entered the room. We stood silent, our breaths held

in her breath denied. Our silence was as the hurricane's
eye, tornadoes swirling around a dead center.

Send her back

to the last ten rows on the bus?
to the end of the line water stinging
behind white men with dogs

straining at leashes teeth tearing?
to the school across the weed-strewn
tracks where broken window

shards stitch like whipped scars?
to servility sustaining white
children while her child alone

at home caresses a hand-me-down
Campbell kid doll one arm missing?
to public auction at the Old Slave Mart,

Charleston, SC, $18 a head, taxed at
three-fifths a free person?
to the lower deck, 4th row of the Aurore,

June 6, 1719, shackled in spoon position
increasing profit from stacked cargo?
to America on the shining hill

our collective conscience
straining at white right when
right becomes wrong

Ida, Cat 4

Sustained winds of 155
the sea spinning tornadoes
surf surge thrown skyward
as the Gulf inhaled barrier islands
riding the Mississippi like a steamship
run aground on snags
wind whining in red and black

screaming like coffin nails driven into
tree trunks amputating branches
I rode a raft
a door I'd found
unhinged
on the second floor
the first floor submerged

and bucked above the churning
sea now unbanked
I passed a church's bell tower
fallen as buttresses eroded
fallen from its celestial height
now crumbling under climate change
I passed above a swirling photo

a wedding day enshrined in gold
a bride and groom in black and white
now turning green in sewage seeping

spillage spooling through New Orleans
where I had walked now sailing steerage
around a doll headless
beside a body bobbing bloated

observed by a lone man
standing on a road's highpoint
his pant legs darkened by the rising rivers
his face darkened by streaks
of grime and etched in
sorrow
like a sculptor scribing graffiti

unearthing loss and trees uprooted
gnarled as fingers thrusting from graves
reaching toward the swollen skies
rain pelting the sodden streets
hundreds dead, thousands missing
amid the flotsam
of lives in wreckage

only a woman in the distance
waist deep in turbulent currents
of houseless chairs and dangling signs
shouting
stop red within the sludge of flood her arms
flailing against the tide her arms upraised in
surrender

The darkness of depth

That summer at Lake Chelan Jack and I the twins and Sue
spent time waterlogged jumping from the remnant pier
its wooden pilings wishing for low tide though August the
water still chill from mountain snow runoff the mountain
our backdrop mist our reprieve from glaring sun and the
future of doubt.

We vied for highest jump biggest splash most dangerous dive
closest to the jagged wood of our pier deepest descent to the
mossy rocks below hidden by the lake's murkiness like all of
life's dangers beneath the surface of placidity.

Sue our daredevil won each frightful dive arching high
diving deep then smiling to gloat at her aversion to danger
beckoning us to compete knowing we'd demur she our
champion who dampened fear like the cold lake's splash on
our sunbaked shoulders.

Cassie my sister sat aside fearing our splashes fearing the
blue-black depth of Lake Chelan's darkness its monsters
unseen coiling to strike the pier's pilings gnarled fingers
thrusting to snare her like a Grimms' tale about the water-nix.

Cassie wore red that day to stop the monsters a sign
signaling us to stay away from her protective distance her
body turned toward the eastern shore where light had fled
near to sand far from fear but metastasis in years to come
reached for her like the pier's clutches and dragged her
beneath the darkness of depth.

Shrill

!shrill, the world screaming
an animal[shredded]
in a steel trap

dead winds stilled:
inverted syntax(airlessly)
gnashing

XXChromosomes
muffled by Y-grinning
teeth

smothering
a child's shriek in phones wincing
wire/cage detention

life unruled in fractured families
speaking tongues in dry blood
beneath brd tweets in leafless trees

Singing the Gun Totin' Blues

a child with a gun shoots a child
(another child another child)

no need to change the gun laws no no
he's just a misunderstood psycho

some hyperactive kid looking for
therapy and increased meds yes yes

what we need is more guns to protect
against more guns NRA bylaw 9 subsection mm

let's arm the teachers a little lady
wearing a reindeer sweater and wreathes

(and a bandolier of double aughts)
when the FBI searched the shooter's home

they found a Christmas photo card
the family posed with their AK 47s

protecting their tinsel tree and
Santa's cookies what kid doesn't need

a new toy a Sig Sauer semi-automatic
the perfect accoutrement to his backpack

stenciled in skulls his god given
2nd amendment right to take lives

in the name of his god given 2nd
amendment right singing don't tread on me

I'll tread on you

The Lord's Prayer, Version 2.0

Our virtual connection,
Digitized be thy name,
Your optimization come,
Your augmentation be done,
Online as it is in cyberspace.
Give us our likes and pins,
Forgive us our clickbait impulses,
As we forgive those who scam, spam, spim and spit,
And tell us what is upworthy,
But deliver us from fake news.
For thine is the algorithm,
The power surge and the A.I.
Forever, until the next app(ocalypse)
Amen.

Dr. Steven M. Gerson, Professor Emeritus, Johnson County Community College, was named 2003-2004 Kansas Professor of the Year, chosen by the Carnegie Foundation. He is the co-author, along with his wife Sharon Gerson, of 13 college-level textbooks and the author of *Once Planed Straight: Poetry of the Prairies* (Spartan Press, 2021). Steve is most proud of his 50+ year marriage to Sharon, for whom all his love poems are written, his wonderful family of Stacy, Stefani, and Rob, and for the joy of spending time with his three grandchildren: Sophia, Samantha, and Jacob. These people are the poetry of Steve's life.

This project was made possible, in part, by generous support from the Osage Arts Community.

Osage Arts Community provides temporary time, space and support for the creation of new artistic works in a retreat format, serving creative people of all kinds — visual artists, composers, poets, fiction and nonfiction writers. Located on a 152-acre farm in an isolated rural mountainside setting in Central Missouri and bordered by ¾ of a mile of the Gasconade River, OAC provides residencies to those working alone, as well as welcoming collaborative teams, offering living space and workspace in a country environment to emerging and mid-career artists. For more information, visit us at www.osageac.org

Osage Arts Community